LOOK IT UP
Now in a fully revised edition

Photo Credits: Heather Angel/Biofotos; Cleveland Museum of Natural History; D. Edwards; Martin F. Glaessner; Michael Holford; Hunterian Museum, Ian Rolfe; Pat Morris; Natural History Photographic Agency; Natural Science Photos; Peabody Museum of Natural History; K.S. Thompson; Polska Akademia Nauk; Royal Society; N.A. Locket; ZEFA.

Front cover: Natural Science Photos.

Illustrators: Fred Anderson; John Sibbick; John Barber; Andrew Skilleter; John Bilham; George Thompson; Jacky Cowdrey; Chris Flynn; Gilchrist Studios; Elizabeth Graham-Yool; Colin Hawkins; Richard Hook; Illustra; Eric Jewell; Angus McBride; David Palmer; Ann Procter.

Chief Educational Adviser
Lynda Snowdon

Teacher Advisory Panel
Helen Craddock, John Enticknap, Arthur Razzell

Editorial Board
Jan Burgess, Rosemary Canter, Philip M. Clark, Beatrice Phillpotts, Sue Seddon, Philip Steele

Picture Researchers
Caroline Adams, Anne Marie Ehrlich, Gayle Hayter, Ethel Hurwicz, Pat Hodgson, Stella Martin, Frances Middlestorb

Designer
Keith Faulkner

Contributors and consultants
John E. Allen, Neil Ardley, Sue Becklake, Robert Burton, Barry Cox, Jacqueline Dineen, David J. Fletcher, Plantagenet Somerset Fry, Bill Gunston, Robin Kerrod, Mark Lambert, Anne Millard, Kaye Orten, Ian Ridpath, Peter Stephens, Nigel Swann, Aubrey Tulley, Tom Williamson, Thomas Wright

Published by Macmillan Children's Books
a division of Macmillan Publishers Limited
4 Little Essex Street, London WC2R 3LF
Associated companies throughout the world

ISBN 0 333 39722 3 (volume 4)
ISBN 0 333 39568 9 (complete set)

Printed in Hong Kong

The Prehistoric World

Second Edition
LOOK IT UP

Contents

UNDERSTANDING FOSSILS

Long, long ago the world was full of many strange animals. Over millions of years new kinds of life evolved. Other animals died out. We know about animals that have died out because remains of their bodies were left in rocks. These remains are called fossils. Here is one way that an animal can become a fossil.

The animal with plate-like spikes on its back is called Stegosaurus. A meat-eating animal has seen it.

Stegosaurus tries to escape from the meat-eating animal. But Stegosaurus cannot run fast. It runs into a river to escape.

The river is deep, and Stegosaurus drowns. Later its body is left on a mud bank in the river. Its flesh decays. Only its skeleton is left.

In the winter, the water rises. It covers the skeleton of Stegosaurus with a thick coat of mud.

More and more layers of mud cover the skeleton. The mud and the bones of Stegosaurus turn into hard rock.

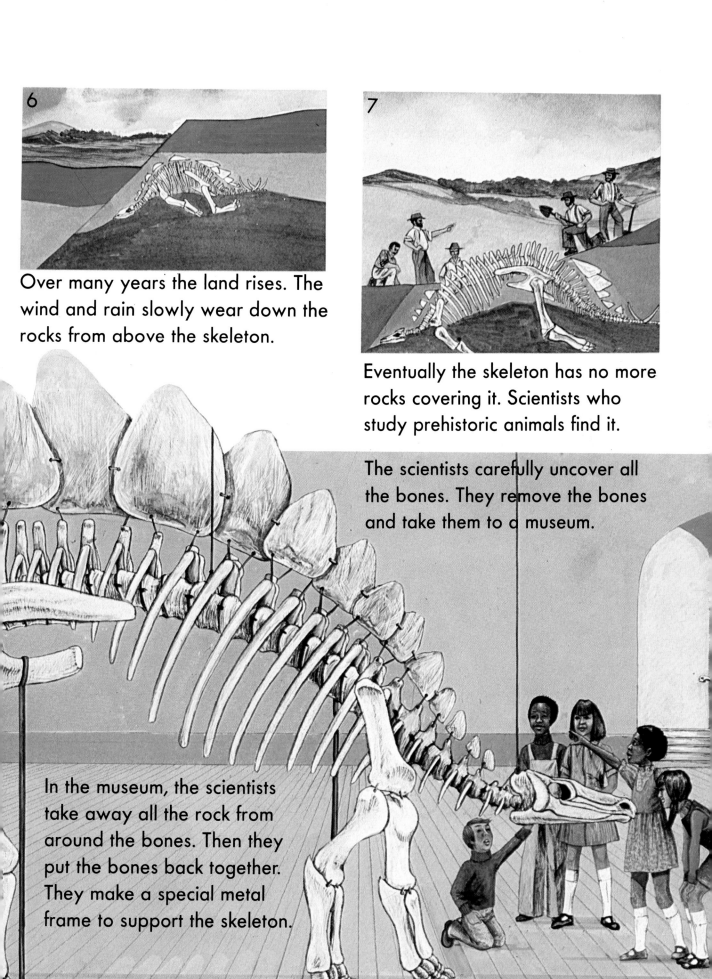

6

Over many years the land rises. The wind and rain slowly wear down the rocks from above the skeleton.

7

Eventually the skeleton has no more rocks covering it. Scientists who study prehistoric animals find it.

The scientists carefully uncover all the bones. They remove the bones and take them to a museum.

In the museum, the scientists take away all the rock from around the bones. Then they put the bones back together. They make a special metal frame to support the skeleton.

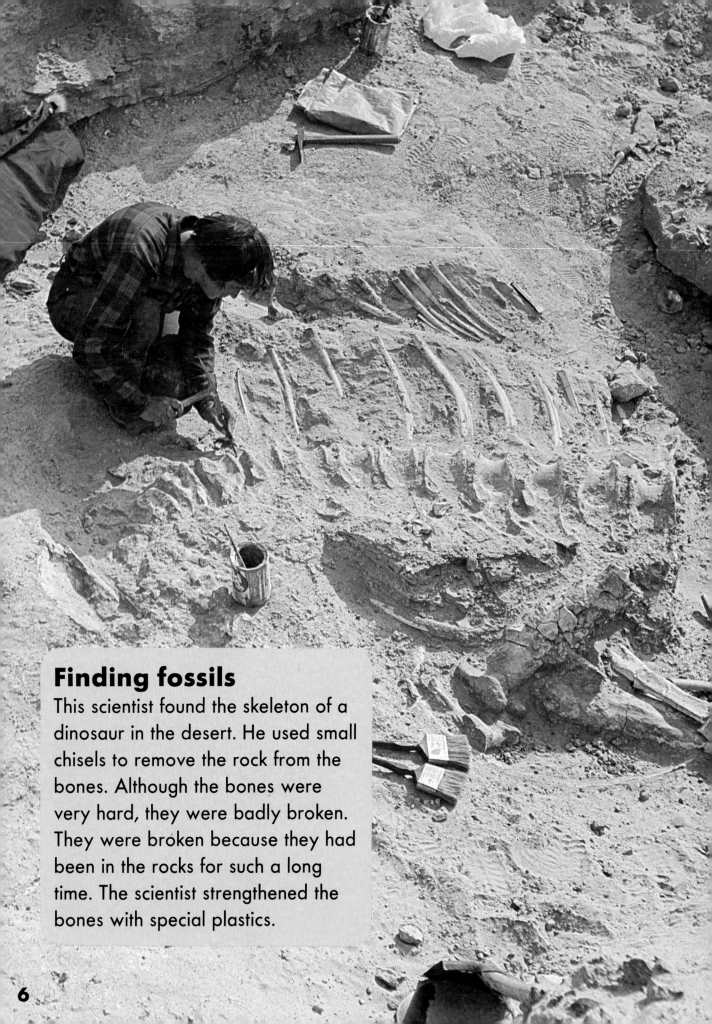

Finding fossils

This scientist found the skeleton of a dinosaur in the desert. He used small chisels to remove the rock from the bones. Although the bones were very hard, they were badly broken. They were broken because they had been in the rocks for such a long time. The scientist strengthened the bones with special plastics.

In prehistoric times, there was a
deep pool of tar in this place. There
was water on the top of the tar.
Animals came to drink the water, and
stuck in the tar. Here are their bones.

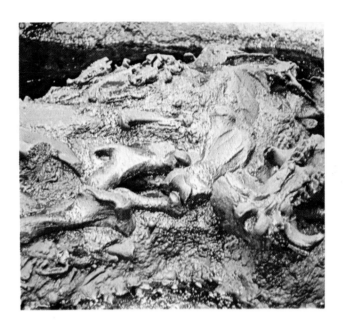

Beaches and cliffs are good places to
find fossils. The sea and the rain
wear away the rocks, and uncover
other rocks. The rocks underneath
are very old. They may contain fossils.

Kinds of fossils

Some fossils are the remains of the hard parts of an animal or plant. Other fossils are only the print of its surface. Very occasionally scientists find a complete little animal that has been trapped in the sticky sap of a tree. It takes millions of years to make a real fossil. But you can easily make copies of fossils.

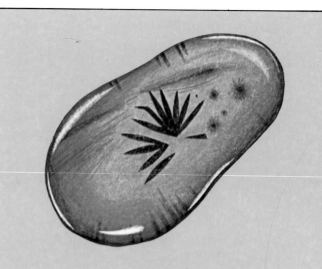

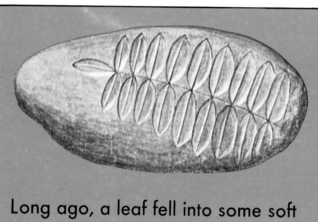

Long ago, a leaf fell into some soft mud. The mud hardened and turned into rock. The leaf print is still clear.

This leaf is preserved in amber. Amber is the sap of trees or plants that has hardened.

You can embed a leaf in clear resin. First half fill the pot with resin.

You can make your own impressions of a leaf by using soft plasticene.

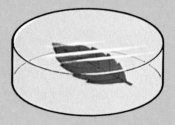

Wait until the resin becomes hard. Then add the leaf and pour the rest of the resin into the pot.

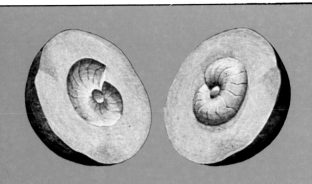

A fossil leaves a hollow or 'mould' in the rock. This can be filled up to give a 'cast' of the fossil.

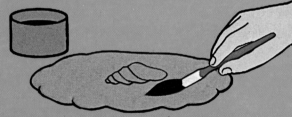

You can push a shell into soft clay to get a mould of its shape.

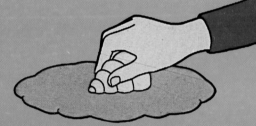

Then paint the clay with water. Now you can pour on some plaster.

Peel the clay away from the dry plaster. You can now see the 'cast'.

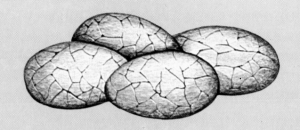

Sometimes we find the fossil eggs of dinosaurs or birds.

You can make your own fossil eggs by using some egg-shaped pebbles.

Pour some plaster over the pebbles and leave it until it sets hard.

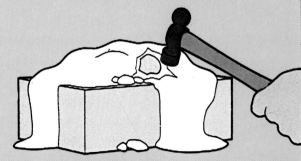

Then carefully chip away some of the plaster. You can see the buried 'eggs'.

What fossils tell us

Sometimes scientists find all the bones of a skeleton connected together. This does not happen very often. Usually they find only a few bones. Often the bones are all jumbled together. You might think that it would be difficult to put all the bones back in the right positions. But really it is easy.

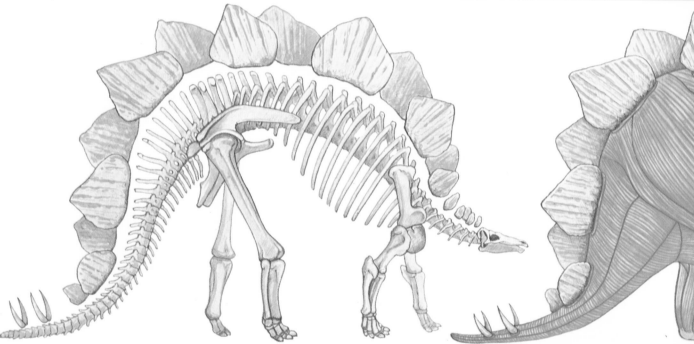

Scientists know that dinosaurs did not have hair or feathers. They know that some dinosaurs had lumps of bone in their skins.

Prints of the skin of dinosaurs show that most dinosaurs had leathery skins. So we can guess what Stegosaurus looked like.

Stegosaurus did not look like this!

Scientists compare the bones they find with the bones of living animals. They can soon tell where each bone belongs. On the bones, scientists can see the marks where the muscles were attached. Then they work out the shape of the body.

Stegosaurus ate plants. It probably had a dull coloured skin, so that meat-eating animals could not see it very easily. Its skin would not have been brightly coloured, but it may have had spots or stripes. Maybe it looked like one of these animals.

EARLY LIFE

The earth probably began as a hot ball of different kinds of gas. Gradually it cooled and became solid. Later still it became cool enough for the steam to turn into water. Only then could living things develop. At first there were only tiny germs. Plants developed later.

gas

plant life begins on land

volcanoes

rain

settled
landscape
and seas

microscopic
pond life

After the plants had appeared,
animal life began. Animals eat plants
or other animals. They can move.

The first plants and animals were
very tiny. They lived in the sea.
Larger plants that could live on land
developed much later.

Early worms and jellyfish

Scientists divide up the history of the earth into different Periods and give a name to each one. The earliest Period is called the Precambrian. We do not know much about the life of that time. But there are lots of fossils from the next Period. This is called the Cambrian Period.

This is one of the oldest animals we know about. It was a jellyfish. It lived in the Precambrian Period.

This worm lived in the Precambrian Period. When it died a cast of its body was left in the mud of the sea.

corals

giant nautiloids

This scene shows the sea life in the
Cambrian Period. This Period came
after the Precambrian Period.
The animals with long bodies and
tentacles are called nautiloids.
Trilobites crawled on the bottom.
Sea urchins lived there too.

jellyfish

sponges

sea
urchins

trilobites

brachiopods

15

Early sea creatures

Many more millions of years passed by. Here is the life of the Silurian Period, about 400 million years ago. The nautiloids now had curved shells. The animal with pincers is called a eurypterid. It was 2 metres long and ate other animals that lived in the sea.

The trilobites crawled on the bottom of the sea, eating the mud. They could roll up into a ball.

sea urchins

nautiloid

brachiopods

The animals on long stalks which you can see in the picture are called sea-lilies. They gathered tiny specks of food from the sea water. During this time, sea creatures made reefs of hard rock. The rock was formed by their skeletons. Today, coral is made in the same way.

Nautiloids that developed later were called ammonites. They filled their shells with gas to float.

eurypterid

sea-lilies

trilobites

Fish with armour

The first fish evolved in the sea over 400 million years ago. Most of them moved very slowly. They had a thick covering of bone on their heads, and on the front part of their bodies. Behind that, they had thick scales. Some fish, like Drepanaspis and Hemicyclaspis, had flat bodies.

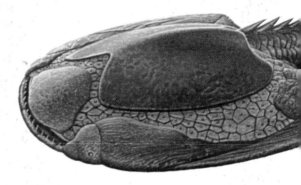

Drepanaspis

Dunkleosteus

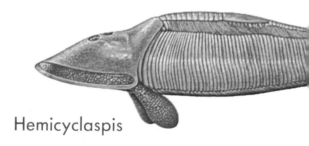

Hemicyclaspis

Pterichthys lived on the bottom of the sea. It pushed itself along with bony flippers. Parexus had several sets of fins and could swim faster. The biggest and most frightening fish was Dunkleosteus. It had strong plates of bone in its large head. These were its 'teeth'. It used them to crunch up the fish that it ate.

Dunkleosteus

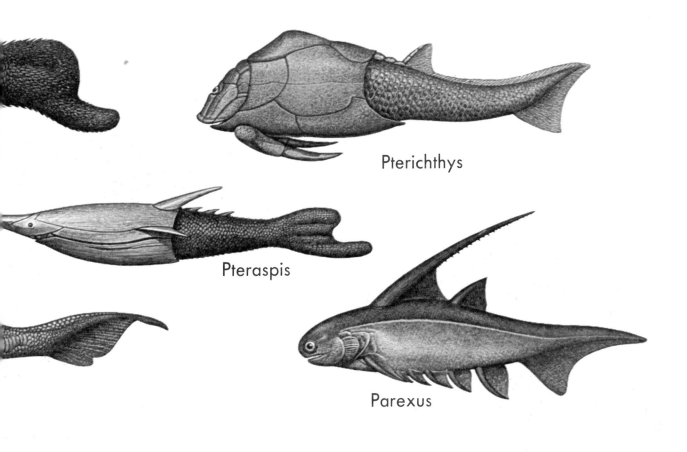

Pterichthys

Pteraspis

Parexus

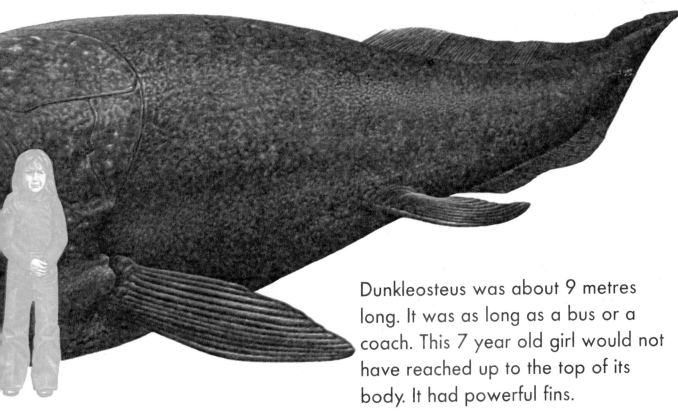

Dunkleosteus was about 9 metres long. It was as long as a bus or a coach. This 7 year old girl would not have reached up to the top of its body. It had powerful fins.

The coelacanth story

The story of the coelacanth is a strange one. Coelacanths were fish with strong muscular fins. Fossils of them have been found in many rocks. But all the rocks they have been found in are at least 65 million years old. Scientists thought that all the coelacanths had died out.

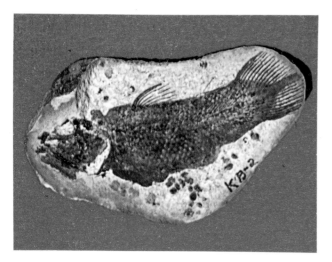

But one day some Africans went fishing. They lived on some islands near Africa. There was a big blue fish among the fish they caught.

1

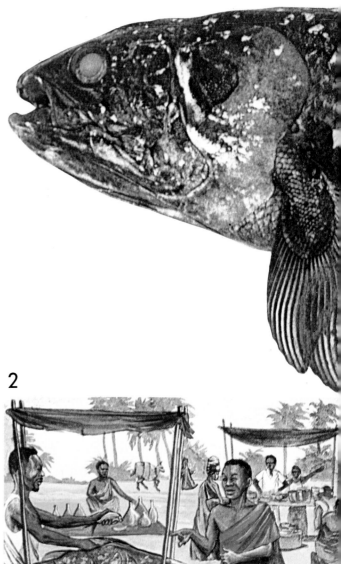

2

The fish was taken to the market to be sold with the others. But a lady called Miss Latimer noticed that one of the fish was very strange. She sent it to a scientist.

Latimeria is quite a big fish. It is nearly 2 metres long. It has a big head and strong fins. Latimeria lives in deep water. This makes it difficult to catch.

4

The scientist realized that the strange fish was a coelacanth. It was the first one to be caught and recognized. It was taken to a museum.

3

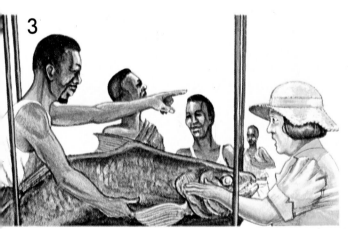

The coelacanth was named Latimeria after the person who took it to the scientist. Now scientists have caught another 50 coelacanths. The fish have been put in museums.

FROM WATER TO LAND

Plants, like animals, found it difficult to live on land. To grow straight, they had to have strong stems. They also had to evolve a waterproof covering so that they did not shrivel up. The pollen of these early plants was carried by the wind. They did not have any flowers like the plants that are alive today.

This is a fossil of the first land plant. It is shown here 12 times bigger than life. It is called Cooksonia.

Today little horsetails grow in marshy places. Millions of years ago plants like these grew into tall trees.

In the big picture you can see some of the early plants.

Psilophyton

Drepanophycus

Rhynia

This living plant is called Psilotum. It looks like the fossil Cooksonia. It lived in warm, tropical places.

Little clubmosses also grew into great trees in the first forests. Protolepidodendron was a fossil clubmoss.

Protolepidodendron

Archaeopteris

Cyclostigma

Early amphibians

Most fish cannot live on land. They cannot breathe air. Their fins are too weak to support their bodies on the ground. But a few fish can wriggle out onto the land, like the little mudskippers in the picture below. Some fish have got lungs. They can breathe air if all the water in the river dries up.

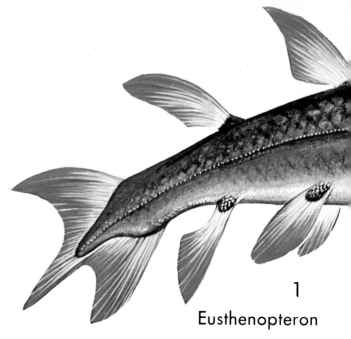

1
Eusthenopteron

3
Ichthyostega

Amphibians can live in the water or on the land. They use their lungs to breathe air. The first amphibians developed from a fish called Eusthenopteron. This fish had lungs and strong fins. Eusthenopteron came onto land to escape from other fish. It found plenty of worms and snails to eat on land.

The first amphibian that scientists know about is called Ichthyostega. It had quite strong limbs instead of fins. It did not have gills. It breathed air instead of water. There must have been a creature half-way between Eusthenopteron and Ichthyostega. Perhaps it looked like this creature on the right.

2

Early swamp life

The first trees grew about 300 million years ago. This Period is called the Carboniferous Period. The trees grew in the warm parts of the world. Many of the trees grew very tall. They grew up to 40 metres high, and lived in steamy swamps.

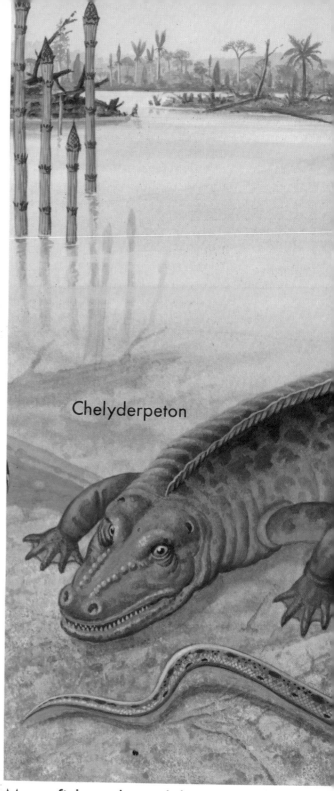

Chelyderpeton

Sometimes we find fossilized tree trunks, like the one in this picture. We call these fossils petrified wood. They often contain bright colours.

Many fish and amphibians lived in the swamps. We sometimes find their bones in coal. All sort of creatures lived in the deep piles of leaves in the forests. The centipede in the picture on the left was 2 metres long.

Dragonfly

Ophiderpeton

The trees dropped their leaves and stems into the water of the swamps. Over millions of years these leaves and stems were pressed tightly together. They dried up and turned into coal.

Under the great trees the ground was covered with thick clumps of ferns. Giant dragonflies flew in the steamy atmosphere. The picture on the left shows the fossil of the leaf of a fern.

Early Texas amphibians

In the Permian Period, about 270 million years ago, many more types of amphibians evolved. The larger ones, like Eryops, lived in the water and ate fish. Archeria had lots of small teeth. It probably ate the smaller animals that lived in the water. The fossils of these amphibians were found in Texas.

Diadectes

Cacops

Some amphibians lived their lives on land. Little Cacops was about 40 centimetres long. It lived on worms and snails. Larger Seymouria probably ate other amphibians. Diadectes had flattened teeth and a bulky body. It was probably the first land animal to eat plants.

Eryops

Seymouria

Diplocaulus

Archeria

This little snake is just hatching out of its egg. The eggs of reptiles have shells. The eggs of amphibians do not have shells.

The tadpole spends its life in the water. It cannot live on land. It breathes through gills. Tadpoles have horny teeth to scrape off food from the plants in the water.

From egg to frog

This is the life cycle of a living amphibian, the frog. The eggs of amphibians only have a covering of jelly. The eggs dry up easily.
So amphibians lay their eggs in water. The jelly stops the eggs clogging together in the water.

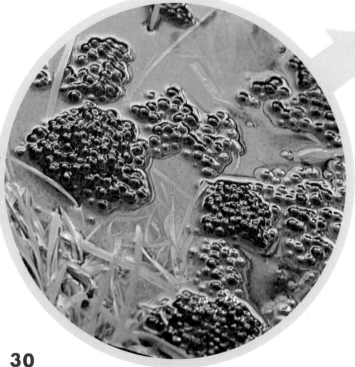

The picture on the left shows a mass of spawn laid in a pond by a frog. Each egg develops into a tadpole. The tadpole wriggles out of the jelly. It uses its long tail to swim, just like a fish.

As it gets bigger, the tadpole gets ready to live on land. Its tail gets shorter. It grows arms and legs. The tadpole's gills get smaller and then disappear. It grows lungs instead, so that it can breathe air.

The adult frog can hop about on land. It can swim in the water too. It feeds on insects and snails. It has a damp skin. The frog breathes both through its skin and through its lungs.

PREHISTORIC REPTILES

Reptiles have an egg with a shell. The egg has its own supply of food and water. The shell protects the baby reptile from being eaten. It does not have to begin life in the water. The reptile lays her eggs on land, not in the water.

The first reptile is called Hylonomus. It lived about 300 million years ago. It looked like a small lizard.

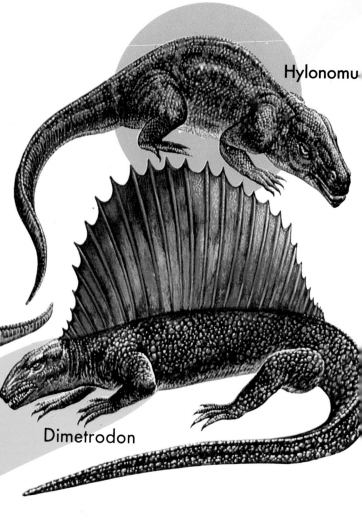

Hylonomu

Dimetrodon

Cynognathus

Erythrotherium

Many different types of reptiles evolved in a short time. Some of them are called mammal-like reptiles. One of them had a strange shape along the top of its back. This may have helped it to get heat from the sun when the animal was cold. These mammal-like reptiles developed into the first mammals.

Reptiles developed in another
important way. They developed into
great dinosaurs.

Euparkeria

Apatosaurus

Stegosaurus

Iguanodon

Tyrannosaurus

There were two groups of dinosaurs.
One group of dinosaurs like
Iguanodon and Stegosaurus ate
plants. The other group included
plant-eaters and meat-eaters.

Triceratops

33

Early dinosaurs

Dinosaurs were the most powerful creatures on earth for 130 million years. Here are some that lived during the Jurassic Period. Apatosaurus and Brachiosaurus were the biggest plant-eating land animals that we know.

Stegosaurus

Apatosaurus

Brachiosaurus

Scelidosaurus

Megalosaurus

Brachiosaurus and Apatosaurus ate
plants. Not all the plant-eating
dinosaurs were giants. Stegosaurus
and Scelidosaurus were smaller. They
had an armour of bone in their skins.
This protected them from the big
meat-eating dinosaurs like great
Megalosaurus.

Later dinosaurs

These dinosaurs lived during the next period of time. It was called the Cretaceous Period. These were the last of the dinosaurs.

Tyrannosaurus

Corythosaurus

Anatosaurus

Styracosaurus

The biggest meat-eating dinosaur we know about lived during this time. It is called Tyrannosaurus and it could run very fast on its back legs. Some of the plant-eating dinosaurs, like Styracosaurus, had horns on their heads. They used the horns to protect themselves from the attacks of meat-eaters.

This picture gives some idea of the size of the large dinosaurs. The head of Tyrannosaurus was about $1\frac{1}{2}$ metres long. Its body measured nearly $14\frac{1}{2}$ metres from head to tail, and it stood over $5\frac{1}{2}$ metres tall.

Dinosaurs and living animals

Dinosaurs were reptiles and laid eggs. They laid the eggs in shallow holes which they dug in the ground. Some nests with 20 eggs have been found. Can you imagine the size of a dinosaur's egg? The biggest egg found was 25 centimetres long. It was as large as 60 chicken's eggs put together.

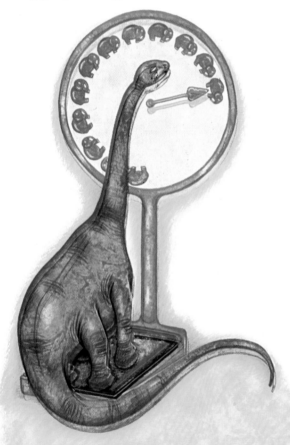

Brachiosaurus was really the dinosaur version of a giraffe. But it was much taller and heavier than a giraffe.

Dinosaurs did not have any hair on their skin. So they quickly became cold when the weather was cool.

The biggest dinosaur of all was Brachiosaurus. It weighed as much as 12 elephants. It had long front legs and a very long neck, so that it could eat the leaves of trees.

It is difficult to imagine the strange world of creatures that have now all died out. Many people think that the dinosaurs were all gigantic. But some of them were quite small. Little Compsognathus was only the size of a chicken.

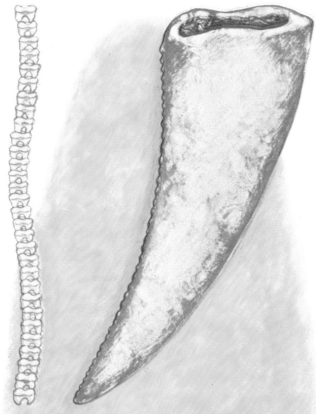

Animals that eat meat have sharp cutting teeth. The teeth of the great Tyrannosaurus were as long as 30 human teeth. Other dinosaurs had hundreds of teeth in the back of their jaws. They used them to grind up the plants they ate.

Sea monsters

While the dinosaurs lived on land, other strange reptiles lived in the seas. Tylosaurus was a relative of the lizard, and ate fish. The largest of the sea reptiles was Kronosaurus. It had a large head. It caught and ate other sea reptiles living in the sea.

Tylosaurus

Plesiosaurs had strong limbs like paddles. They used these to push themselves through the water. Some of them had long rubbery necks. Some Plesiosaurs ate fish.

Kronosaurus

Ichthyosaurs swam like fish. They lashed their tails from side to side. They had a fin on their backs. Their long snout hid many teeth. They used it to catch and eat fish. These reptiles only had small limbs.

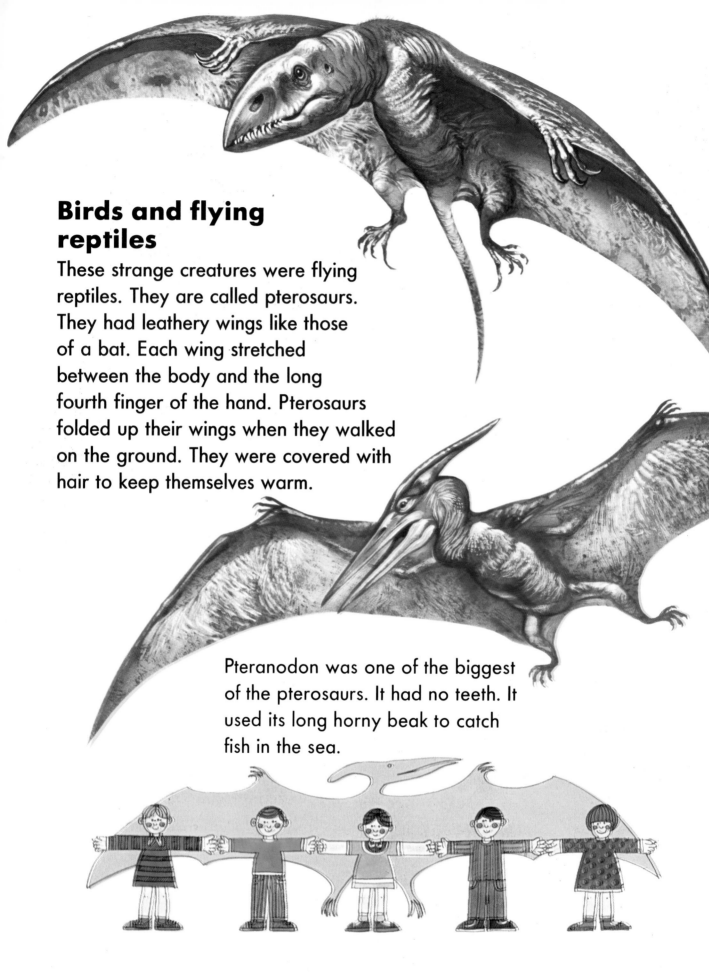

Birds and flying reptiles

These strange creatures were flying reptiles. They are called pterosaurs. They had leathery wings like those of a bat. Each wing stretched between the body and the long fourth finger of the hand. Pterosaurs folded up their wings when they walked on the ground. They were covered with hair to keep themselves warm.

Pteranodon was one of the biggest of the pterosaurs. It had no teeth. It used its long horny beak to catch fish in the sea.

Rhamphorhynchus was only the size of a sparrow. It had sharp teeth and ate insects. Its long tail ended in a little rudder. It used this to steer itself through the air.

Archaeopteryx was the first bird. Its body was covered with feathers. But it had a long bony tail like a reptile. Archaeopteryx also still had teeth in its beak. The fingers on its wings had little claws.

Early birds

Birds have a covering of feathers.
So they are always warm. Like
reptiles, they lay eggs. The eggs are
laid in a nest and the parent birds
keep them warm. Most birds can fly.
This means that they can make their
nests in high places like trees.
But some birds like the penguin and
the ostrich are no longer able to fly.

Birds could escape from enemies on
the ground by flying away.
Sometimes they landed in places
where there were no fierce enemies.

Phororhachos lived in South America.
It had a head as big as a horse's
head, and strong feet with claws.

Hesperornis was a bird that lived at
the same time as the dinosaurs.
It could not fly. Instead, it used its
strong hind limbs to swim in the sea.
It used its sharp teeth to catch fish.

Birds no longer needed to fly to stay alive. So those that could not fly could survive. Over millions of years the birds gradually changed.

Their legs grew longer to run about. Their wings grew smaller. The birds got bigger and fiercer. Sometimes they ate other animals.

The moa was over 3 metres tall. It lived on plant food. People hunted this animal until it died out.

When the dinosaurs died out, there were no large mammals that ate other animals. But some big meat-eating birds developed. Diatryma was one of these. It was taller than a man.

The end of the dinosaurs

All the dinosaurs died out at about the same time. We still do not know why this happened. Some people think new types of plants evolved. The new plants might have contained juices that poisoned the dinosaurs. But we know some of the dinosaurs evolved after these plants. So they must have been used to eating them.

Other people think that the world became hotter and hotter. The big dinosaurs would not have been able to find shady places to keep cool. But the small dinosaurs died out too.

Perhaps the dinosaurs all died out because the world got too cold. But then they would have been able to survive in the hotter parts. Before the dinosaurs died out, the temperature was the same all through the year. Then it changed. The summer became hotter and the winter colder. Perhaps the dinosaurs could not live with these changes.

The dinosaurs were reptiles, and laid eggs. Did the little mammals eat their eggs? Was that why the dinosaurs died out? But the mammals and dinosaurs had lived together for millions of years. So we still cannot be sure why the dinosaurs all died.

THE FIRST MAMMALS

After the dinosaurs died out, the little mammals spread throughout the world. Mammals are different from reptiles. They usually do not lay eggs. Instead, the young mammal grows for a long time inside its mother's body. After it is born, it feeds on its mother's milk. Mammals are covered with hair to keep warm.

Mammals are more clever than reptiles or birds. They can learn many things. Young mammals stay with their parents. The parents teach them how to find food and how to keep away from danger. Some families of mammals stay in groups. They protect themselves from enemies.

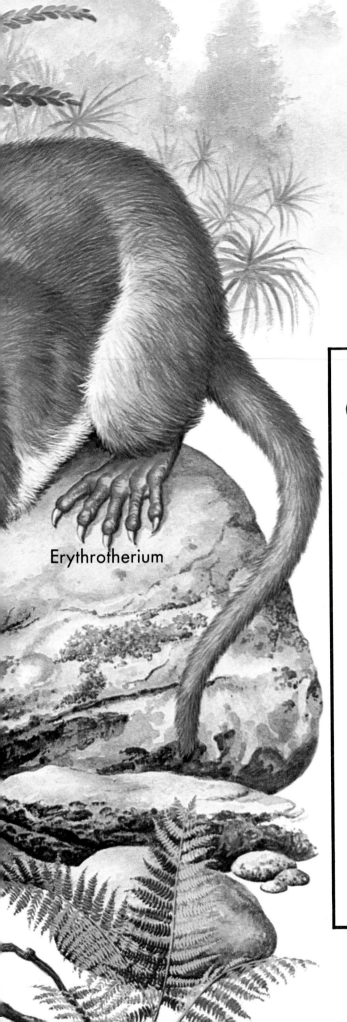
Erythrotherium

The first mammals evolved when the dinosaurs were still alive. They were only small. They fed on insects, snails and lizards. Little Erythrotherium was one of the first mammals. Many new types of mammals developed after the dinosaurs died out. They grew much bigger. Some fed on meat, others ate only plants.

Bats are mammals that can fly. Their hands have changed into wings.

Dolphins, whales and seals are mammals that live in the sea.

The platypus is one of the very few living mammals that still lays eggs.

The first elephants

Elephants have evolved an easy way to reach the leaves on tall trees. Their upper lip has grown into a long flexible trunk. They can use the trunk to pull down branches from trees. Elephants are also strong enough to push down small trees. They do this so that they can eat the leaves more comfortably.

Moeritherium was the first elephant. It was only the size of a pig. It had a very short trunk.

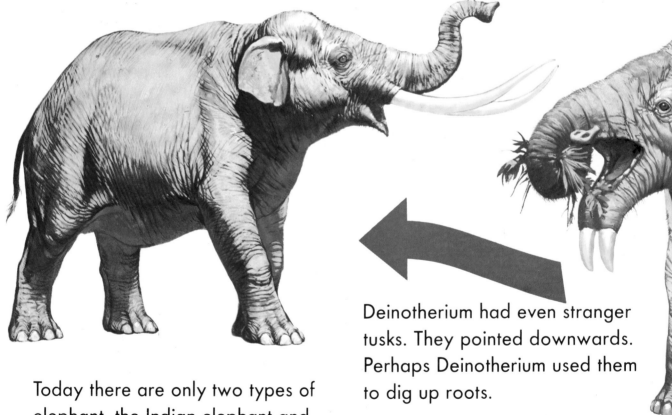

Deinotherium had even stranger tusks. They pointed downwards. Perhaps Deinotherium used them to dig up roots.

Today there are only two types of elephant, the Indian elephant and the African. The Indian elephant you can see here has a domed head. It has ears which are much smaller than the African elephant's ears.

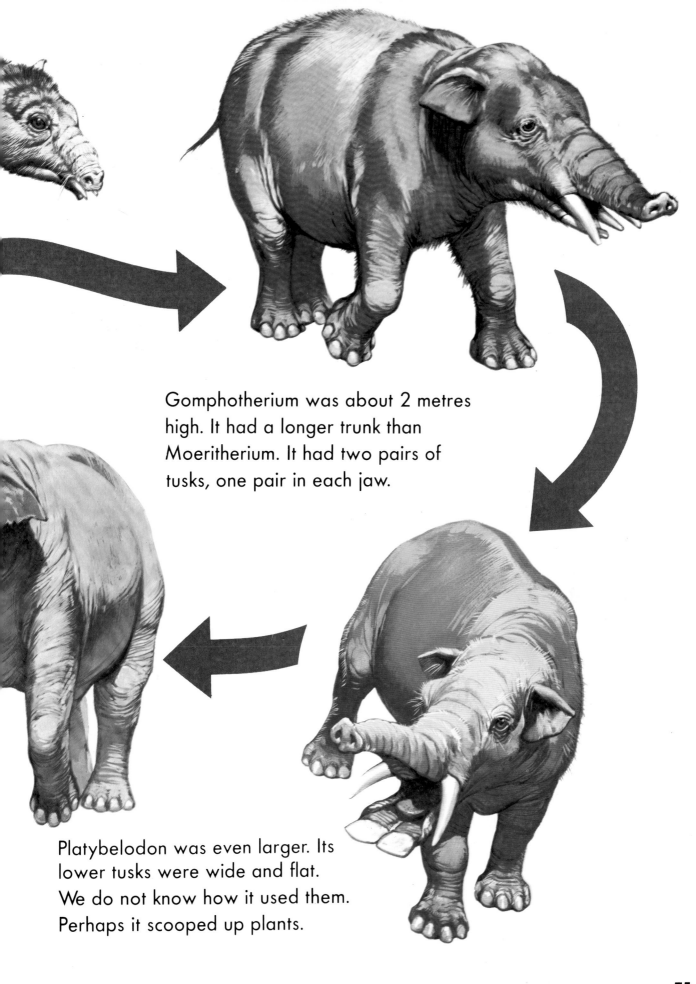

Gomphotherium was about 2 metres
high. It had a longer trunk than
Moeritherium. It had two pairs of
tusks, one pair in each jaw.

Platybelodon was even larger. Its
lower tusks were wide and flat.
We do not know how it used them.
Perhaps it scooped up plants.

Strange mammals

Many strange types of mammal lived in the past. Some had horns to defend themselves. Some mammals were bigger than any land animal alive today. Synthetoceras had a long horn on its nose. The horn ended in two sharp points. It had horns in front of its ears, too.

Indricotherium is the biggest land mammal that ever lived. Its shoulders were nearly 6 metres above the ground. Its head was 1½ metres long. It ate the leaves of trees.

The first horse was only the size of a dog. It is called Hyracotherium. It lived in forests and fed on the leaves of trees and bushes.

Horses gradually became bigger and bigger. They moved out onto the grasslands to eat grass. The ground there was harder than in the forests.

Uintatherium ate plants. It was
4 metres long. There were strange
bony lumps on its head and jaws.
These may have protected it from
the attacks of meat-eating animals.

Smilodon was a very fierce meat
eater. It had long sharp fangs. It used
these to bite through the thick skins
of the animals it hunted. It only
hunted the animals that ate plants.

On the hard ground, horses did not
need such big feet as they did on the
soft earth of the forests. Their feet
became smaller and lighter.

Today horses only have a single toe
and a hoof on each foot. They have
big strong teeth so that they can eat
the hard grass.

THE EVOLUTION OF MAN

Today scientists know a great deal about the development of early man. Long, long ago, our ancestors spent a lot of their time in the trees. But they could also walk on the ground.

Proconsul

Ramapithecus

Australopithecus

Leakey's man

Over millions of years, man began to spend more time on the ground.

His body became straighter, and gradually he was able to run faster.

This picture is of a great valley in Africa called the Olduvai Gorge. Many fossils of early man have been found here. The ancestors of man had to leave their life in the trees because the climate was changing. The weather was becoming colder and the forests were becoming smaller. Instead, there were scattered trees and grassland. Our ancestors lived and found food there.

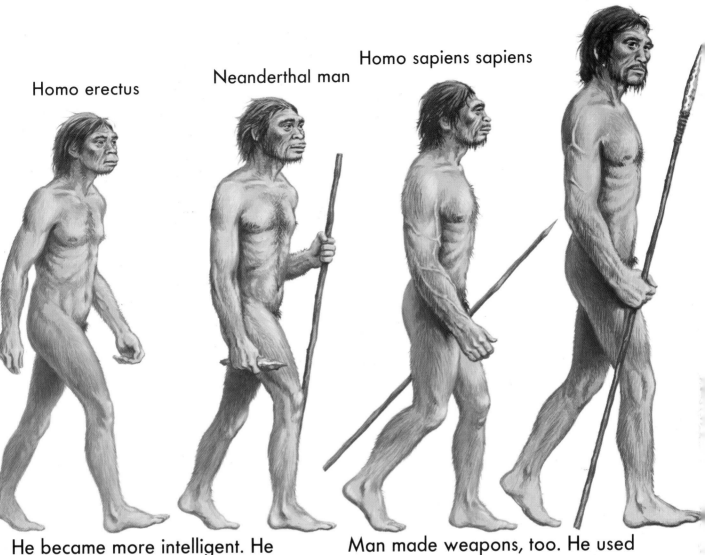

Homo sapiens sapiens

Neanderthal man

Homo erectus

He became more intelligent. He made tools out of stone and wood.

Man made weapons, too. He used them to hunt animals.

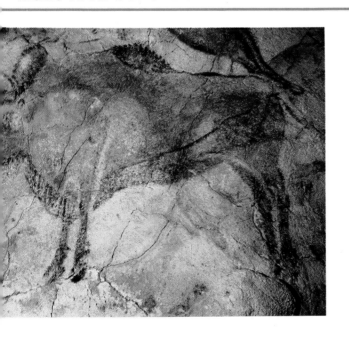

Man had learned to draw and paint long before he lived in towns. He carved designs on his bone tools. His beautiful paintings can be seen on the walls of ancient caves. The paintings and the carvings show the animals that early man was hunting. The artist may have drawn them to bring luck in the next day's hunting. They may also have been part of his magic and religion.

Australopithecus

Australopithecus was about 120 centimetres tall and walked almost upright. His brain was quite small and he had a face like an ape.

Australopithecus probably ate anything he could find. He collected fruit and berries, chased lizards and mice, and chewed on bones.

He hunted in groups to catch bigger animals. Australopithecus probably used animal bones as weapons. He made simple stone tools. He sheltered in caves during bad weather.

Leakey's man

Early man was not a common creature so the bones of fossil men are not often found. But we know that man continued to evolve. Dr Leakey recently discovered a type of fossil man which nobody knew about before. Now that man has learnt to grow his own food crops, he is one of the commonest animals.

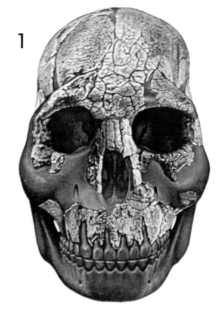

1

This shows how we reconstruct the newly discovered fossils of early men. First, the scientist joins the fragments of the skull together.

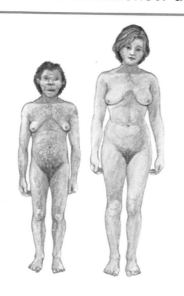

As mankind evolved, the size of adult people increased. They grew bigger because they found more things to eat. Bigger people could run faster to escape from their enemies.

Dr Leakey's man lived in places where there were many lakes. He may have lived on fish as well as other animals. He built low shelters of stones to keep out the wind.

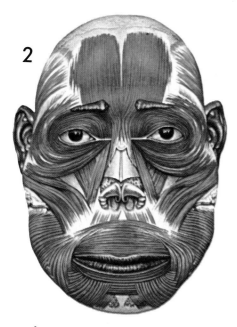

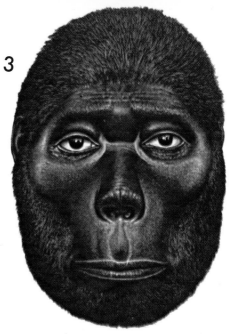

Then the scientist reconstructs the muscles of the face. These muscles moved the eyebrows, lips and jaws. The ears and nose are added, too.

Finally the scientist covers the face with skin and hair. Of course, we do not know the colour of the skin, or how much hair there was.

Homo erectus

The type of man who lived before modern man is called Homo erectus. He lived about 1½ million years ago. He was bigger and more intelligent than Australopithecus. Homo erectus learnt to use fire. He used it to cook his food. The fire protected him from wild animals, and kept him warm.

Once people began to live in large groups, they must have learned to use words. These were probably only noises at first, to warn of danger or to call each other. Gradually they learned to use a special noise or word for each animal they hunted. This is how language began.

Neanderthal man

After Homo erectus the next type of man was called Neanderthal man. He had heavy ridges over his eyes, and a sloping chin and forehead. But his brain was as big as ours. He made many different types of stone tools. Neanderthal man hunted animals like the aurochs. Their skins kept him warm during the winter.

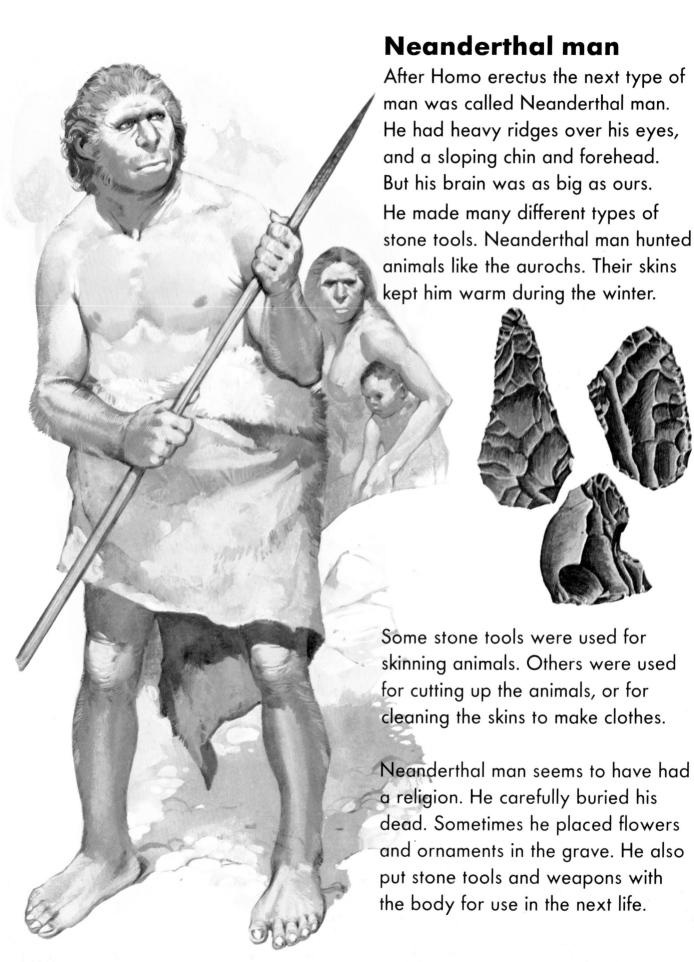

Some stone tools were used for skinning animals. Others were used for cutting up the animals, or for cleaning the skins to make clothes.

Neanderthal man seems to have had a religion. He carefully buried his dead. Sometimes he placed flowers and ornaments in the grave. He also put stone tools and weapons with the body for use in the next life.

Some people think there is a monster living in a lake in Scotland. They call it the Loch Ness monster. If it is there it is probably a Plesiosaur. It is a living fossil.

In 1853 a giant model was made of an Iguanodon. It was made for the Crystal Palace Exhibition. A dinner was given inside the Iguanodon for 21 people.

Tanystropheus lived in the sea. It used its long neck to catch fish. But when Tany was only young it lived on the land. Some scientists think it may have caught insects.

Pachycephalosaurs had very thick skulls. They were just like helmets. Sometimes the male animals had fights. Then they banged their heads together to see who was stronger.

INDEX